Looga and Barooga
The Treasure of Soap Island

Written by
Robin Etherington

Illustrated by
Zak Simmonds-Hurn

OXFORD
UNIVERSITY PRESS

OXFORD
UNIVERSITY PRESS

Great Clarendon Street, Oxford, OX2 6DP, United Kingdom

Oxford University Press is a department of the University of Oxford. It furthers the University's objective of excellence in research, scholarship, and education by publishing worldwide. Oxford is a registered trade mark of Oxford University Press in the UK and in certain other countries

Text © Robin Etherington 2015
Illustrations © Zak Simmonds-Hurn 2015

The moral rights of the author have been asserted

First published 2015

British Library Cataloguing in Publication Data
Data available

ISBN: 978-0-19-835640-0

10 9 8 7 6 5 4 3 2 1

Paper used in the production of this book is a natural, recyclable product made from wood grown in sustainable forests. The manufacturing process conforms to the environmental regulations of the country of origin.

Printed in China by Hing Yip

Acknowledgements

Series Advisor: Nikki Gamble

6

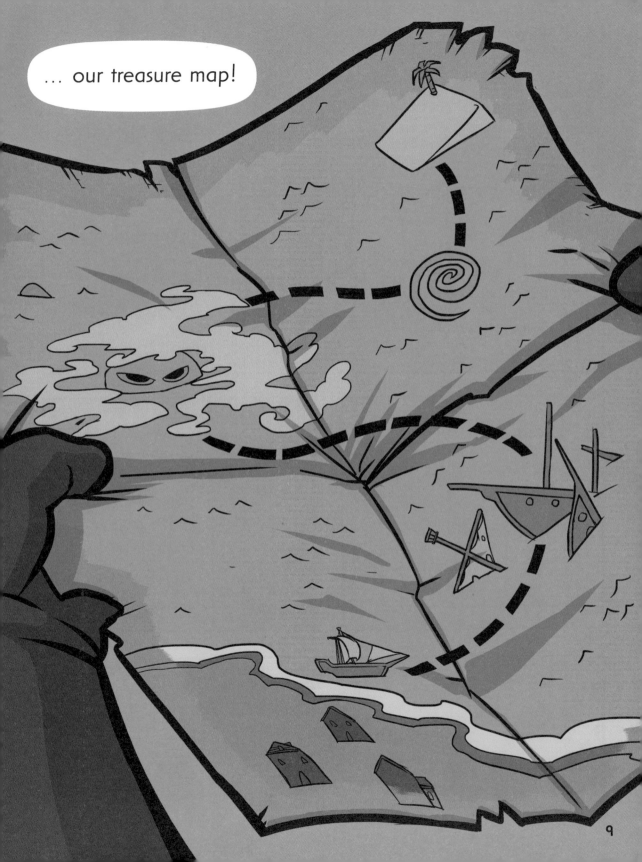

Wow! Look at all those tentacles! How many are there?

Eight ... and they've given me an idea.

19

23

The end!